Cosmos, Earth and Mankind Astronomy for Kids Vol II

Astronomy & Space Science

Speedy Publishing LLC
40 E. Main St. #1156
Newark, DE 19711
www.speedypublishing.com

Space and time began with a massive event. Scientists describe it in the Big Bang Theory.

Pythagoras, Copernicus, Newton, Kepler, Einstein, Hubble, and Hawking contributed great discoveries about the universe.

Our planet Earth is a wonderful place to live in. Earth is the only planet that we know of that has living things.

Other planets in our Solar System are uninhabitable. We are very fortunate that we live in a world that sustains life with a temperature that is totally different from that of other planets.

Aside from the facts that we know about our planet, there are still many discoveries that we need to know to fully understand the entire universe.

Have you ever heard of the Steady State Theory?

This theory was first suggested by Herman Bondi and Thomas Gold in 1948.

Fred Hoyle and others extended this theory in 1949 as an alternative to the Big Bang Theory.

According to the Steady State Theory, the universe is expanding but its average density is constant because of the continuous creation of matter.

In this theory, a universe that is in steady-state has no beginning and no end in time.

The steady state theory ran into problems in the 1950s, when there were many observations and evidence that contradicted the theory.

Many scientists supported the Big Bang Theory instead of the Steady State Theory.

DARK ENERGY

In 1998, this repulsive force was discovered by two teams of astronomers, including Adam Riess, Saul Perlmutter, and Brian Schmidt.

They measured the light coming from Type IA supernovae, also known as standard candles.

The brightness of these exploding stars was consistent.

They noticed that the brightness of more distant exploding stars was fainter.

So they concluded that the expansion of the universe was accelerating.

Then the team suggested that a substance they called dark energy was causing the expansion of the universe to accelerate. The universe began accelerating about 5 billion years ago.

What the astronomers observed was the first evidence of dark energy in the universe.

Do you know the great contributions of Sir Frederick William Herschel?

He was a German astronomer who discovered the planet Uranus in 1781 using a telescope.

He noticed in the sky that there was a star that seemed different from the other stars.

So he observed it many times and saw that it revolved around the Sun.

The planet's orbit was about 18 times farther from the Sun compared to Earth's orbit.

He also discovered the moons of Uranus, which have been named Titania and Oberon.

He is the one who developed the Theory of Stellar Evolution. His thinking about stars received a surprise when he observed a nebula on November 13, 1790. He interpreted a nebula as a central star that is surrounded by a luminous fluid. This discovery was in contrast to his earlier views.

Herschel reasoned out that those nebulae might be distant island galaxies.

He then concluded that due to gravity the central star condensed out the clouds surrounding it.

These amazing discoveries gave us a glimpse of how the universe began.

We are still learning, as our scientists to discover valuable information about our universe.

www.ingramcontent.com/pod-product-compliance
Lightning Source LLC
LaVergne TN
LVHW080045170826
845677LV00024B/1622

* 9 7 9 8 8 6 9 4 4 3 1 8 2 *